SNAKES SET II

CORAL SNAKES

Adam G. Klein
ABDO Publishing Company

visit us at
www.abdopub.com

Published by ABDO Publishing Company, 4940 Viking Drive, Edina, Minnesota 55435.
Copyright © 2006 by Abdo Consulting Group, Inc. International copyrights reserved in all
countries. No part of this book may be reproduced in any form without written permission from
the publisher. The Checkerboard Library™ is a trademark and logo of ABDO Publishing
Company.

Printed in the United States.

Cover Photo: Corbis
Interior Photos: Animals Animals pp. 5, 6, 10, 14; Corbis pp. 8, 9, 11, 13, 15, 17, 19, 21;
    Peter Arnold p. 7

Series Coordinator: Megan Murphy
Editors: Stephanie Hedlund, Megan Murphy
Art Direction & Maps: Neil Klinepier

Library of Congress Cataloging-in-Publication Data

Klein, Adam G., 1976-
    Coral snakes / Adam G. Klein.
        p. cm. -- (Snakes. Set II)
    Includes index.
    ISBN 1-59679-280-9 *1697*
        1. Coral snakes--Juvenile literature. I. Title.

QL666.O64K59 2005
597.96'44--dc22

                                                                          2005040397

CONTENTS

CORAL SNAKES

There are 11 different **families** of snakes. Coral snakes belong to the Elapidae family. Members of this family have a pair of short, fixed fangs at the front of their upper jaw. Coral snakes are small and **venomous**. However, they are rarely deadly.

Today, there are more than 50 species of coral snakes in North and South America. There are also some species in Africa, Asia, and Australia. Early North American explorers named coral snakes. They thought these snakes were as colorful as coral on the ocean floor!

Snakes are reptiles. Like all reptiles, snakes have scaly skin. They shed their skin several times a year. Snakes are also cold-blooded. This means they rely on an outside energy source, such as the sun, for warmth.

This coral snake species is found in the rain forests of Costa Rica. Its Latin name is Micrurus nigrocinctus.

SIZES

Coral snakes have narrow heads, slender bodies, and long, pointed tails. Their noses are rounded and their eyes are small.

Overall, coral snakes are relatively small. An average coral snake is 18 to 30 inches (46 to 76 cm) long. But, the length of a coral snake depends on the species.

This coral snake lives in Belize in Central America.

Coral snakes are small and can hide easily in grass or under rocks.

The western coral snake is usually less than 20 inches (50 cm) long. It doesn't grow much wider than a pencil. The eastern coral snake is larger. It is usually 24 to 30 inches (61 to 76 cm) long. However, one of the South American species can be four feet (1 m) long.

COLORS

Coral snakes are brightly colored and have smooth, shiny scales. Most species have bodies that are ringed with red, black, and yellow bands. Sometimes the yellow bands are white instead. But, the snake's nose is always black.

The coral snake's bright coloration serves as a warning to **predators** that it is poisonous. It is telling its enemies to stay away. This works so well that some

nonvenomous snakes **mimic** the pattern to protect themselves, too.

Because the coral snake is poisonous, it is important to be able to tell it apart from other

This nonvenomous tropical king snake mimics the colorful banding of the coral snake.

snakes. If red stripes touch black stripes, the snake is probably safe. But if red stripes touch yellow stripes, it could be a coral snake.

There is even a poem to help you remember how to identify a coral snake:

> *Red touching yellow, kill a fellow,*
>
> *Red touching black, poisons lack.*

The coral snake's distinctive band pattern is seen here. But when in doubt, it is wise to just leave a snake alone.

WHERE THEY LIVE

The coral snake is found in a variety of **habitats**. Some species prefer grasslands or dry desert regions with rocky or sandy soil. Other species like **humid** or tropical forest regions. Coral snakes also live in marshy areas near ponds or streams.

Coral snakes are shy and secretive. They are burrowers, so they are not often seen above ground.

Coral snakes spend most of their time in animal tunnels, in hollow logs, or under rocks. They like to hide under leaf litter on forest floors, too.

These snakes are primarily **nocturnal**. But, they can be found prowling in the early morning or early evening hours. They also often appear after it rains.

An eastern coral snake

The coral snake lives in warm or tropical climates. So, it does not need to lay in the sun to keep warm like some other species.

WHERE THEY ARE FOUND

Most coral snakes are found in North and South America. The two most common species are the western and eastern coral snakes.

The western coral snake lives in the Sonoran Desert of Arizona and northern Mexico. It is found in the lower elevations of southwestern New Mexico as well. The western coral snake is also called the Arizona coral snake or the Sonoran coral snake.

NORTH AMERICA

Atlantic Ocean

Pacific Ocean

SOUTH AMERICA

Where Coral Snakes Live

The eastern coral snake is found in the southeastern United States. It lives as far north as North Carolina, and as far south as Mexico. It is also highly concentrated in Florida. The eastern coral snake is sometimes called the Texas coral snake or the harlequin coral snake.

There are also several coral snake species in Central and South America. They are usually larger, and their bite is more likely to be deadly. Some South American

The African and Asian coral snakes, like this blue Malaysian coral snake, are often called false coral snakes. They have similar bodies and habits, but they are not related to any of the American species.

coral snakes have wide red rings and smaller black rings bordered with narrow yellow bands.

SENSES

Like most other animals, coral snakes are just trying to survive. In order to do this, snakes have to use their natural abilities. They do not sense things in

A coral snake keeps its head close to the ground as it slithers around.

the same way people do. Coral snakes have their own way to experience the world.

Coral snakes have large, round eyes but very poor vision. Since they don't see well, coral snakes find their way by smell and vibrations.

A snake picks up a smell with its tongue. Then, it deposits the scent particles on the roof of its mouth. A snake's mouth contains a Jacobson's organ. This special organ acts like the human nose. It helps the snake figure out what smells are in the air.

Snakes sense sound in an unusual way, too. They do not have ears and cannot hear. Instead, they feel sound vibrations through bones in their jaw. These vibrations help them sense movement nearby. This way they can find their next meal or avoid a possible **predator**.

Coral snakes are not seen above ground very often. They use their senses to hide from humans and predators.

DEFENSE

The coral snake is **venomous**, but it still has some **predators**. Several mammals, such as foxes and coyotes, are known to eat this snake. Birds of prey and larger snakes eat them, too.

A coral snake defends itself in several ways. Its bright colors are intended to warn away predators. If that doesn't work, a coral snake sticks up its tail. It also makes a popping noise with the lining of its **cloaca**.

If the snake continues to feel threatened, it strikes out. The coral snake has a **neurotoxic** venom. This poison can cause **paralysis**, **respiratory** failure, or possibly death to its enemy.

However, very few human deaths have been reported from a coral snake bite. This is because these snakes have extremely short fangs. Their fangs are less than one-quarter inch (6 mm) long. So, they are often not long enough to penetrate human skin.

If a person is bitten, it is important to seek out **antivenin** treatment. Coral snakes produce smaller amounts of **venom** due to their size. But, their venom can still be deadly.

Coral snakes are less aggressive than other snakes in the Elapidae family.

FOOD

Like most snakes, coral snakes swallow their food whole. But, coral snakes cannot open their mouths very wide to swallow larger prey. So, they normally eat animals that are smaller than they are.

A coral snake's favorite meals are other small snakes. They also eat lizards, fish, and **amphibians**. When hunting, a coral snake will quickly strike its prey. Within a moment, the snake's poison will be **injected** into its target.

But, the coral snake's injection method is not as effortless as other poisonous snakes. Its fangs are short, so it must hold on to its victim and chew in order to penetrate the skin. A coral snake often stays attached to its victim until it is completely **paralyzed**.

Opposite page: *This Arizona, or western, coral snake is eating a crowned snake.*

BABIES

Coral snakes are the only poisonous snake in North America to lay eggs. Mother snakes often choose places such as rotting wood, underground burrows, or rock piles to lay their eggs. The female coral snake lays 2 to 13 eggs in the summer.

After about 70 to 90 days, the eggs are ready to hatch. It can take up to four hours for a baby coral snake to escape from the shell. At birth, the coral snake is only seven to eight inches (18 to 20 cm) long. They are **venomous** upon hatching.

As coral snakes grow, they shed their skin. They double their size in less than two years. By three years of age, they are usually fully grown. These snakes can live 20 to 30 years in the wild.

A baby coral snake hatches from its egg.

GLOSSARY

amphibian - an animal that can live in the water and on land. Frogs, toads, and salamanders are amphibians.

antivenin - a kind of medicine used to reverse the effects of a poisonous snakebite.

cloaca (kloh-AY-kuh) - the chamber in a snake that waste and reproductive products pass through before leaving the body.

family - a group that scientists use to classify similar plants or animals. It ranks above a genus and below an order.

habitat - a place where a living thing is naturally found.

humid - having moisture or dampness in the air.

inject - to forcefully introduce a fluid into the body, usually with a needle or something sharp.

mimic - to imitate or copy.

neurotoxic - harmful to the nervous system of the body.

nocturnal (nahk-TUHR-nuhl) - active at night.

paralyze (PEHR-uh-lize) - to cause a loss of motion or feeling in a part of the body.

predator - an animal that kills and eats other animals.

respiratory - having to do with the system of organs involved with breathing.

venom - a poison produced by some animals and insects. It usually enters a victim through a bite or sting.

WEB SITES

To learn more about coral snakes, visit ABDO Publishing Company on the World Wide Web at **www.abdopub.com**. Web sites about these snakes are featured on our Book Links page. These links are routinely monitored and updated to provide the most current information available.

INDEX